Acknowledgements/Publication Notes

This is the first edition of the *Best Practices for the Retrieval of Video Evidence from Digital CCTV Systems* representing a joint project undertaken by the Federal Bureau of Investigation, Operational Technology Division, Digital Evidence Section, Forensic Audio, Video and Image Analysis Unit in conjunction with the Technical Support Working Group and the National Terrorism Preparedness Institute at St. Petersburg College. The committee brought together a variety of law enforcement representatives who are experts in the retrieval of video evidence from Digital Closed Circuit Television Systems.

Special thanks go to these agencies for their time and effort.

Combating Terrorism Technology Support Office, Technical Support Working Group
Department of Forensic Science – Commonwealth of Virginia
Federal Bureau of Investigation
Home Office Scientific Development Branch, UK
Los Angeles Police Department
Metropolitan Police Department, UK
National Terrorism Preparedness Institute, at St. Petersburg College
New York City Police Department
United States Secret Service

The information in this guide is for informational purposes only and does not constitute legal advice. The information may not reflect the most current legal developments; therefore, it is always advised to consult your local counsel regarding any question you may have.

Officer Safety

As in any criminal investigation **officer safety is paramount** and should take precedence over any information contained within this document. The situation often perceived in crimes related to technology may not appear threatening; Law Enforcement investigators should not become complacent with individuals or their environment, including investigations of crimes related to technology.

Although technology brings forth new types of criminal activity it also provides new methods and tools to aid in the successful apprehension and prosecution of the individual(s) engaged in these activities.

The purpose of a criminal investigation is to provide unbiased evidence and facts in order to solve a crime and bring the guilty parties to justice. This can be aided through the proper collection, preservation and processing of the pertinent evidence in the case.

Terminology

Highlighted terms and acronyms are defined in the glossary at the end of this guide. It is recommended that you familiarize yourself with the glossary before using this guide.

Purpose

The purpose of this guide is to provide the best methods for the retrieval of video data evidence from Digital Closed Circuit Television (DCCTV) recording systems.

These best practices, guidelines and recommendations are intended to provide responding Law Enforcement personnel guidance in securing and collecting video data from DCCTV systems. This will ensure that best methods are utilized to retrieve the recorded data and maintain its integrity.

The retrieved video data should be retained as the master evidence. Whenever possible, the native/proprietary recorded video data from the DCCTV recording system should be retrieved to maintain the integrity and image quality of the evidence.

These guidelines are meant to inform agencies of the best practices for DCCTV retrieval and to aid in the development of Standard Operating Procedures (SOPs). These practices should be used in conjunction with current agency policies.

Scope

This document is intended to provide procedures for the collection of digital video that ensure playback while maintaining best evidence. DCCTV retrieval is the collection of relevant video data and associated metadata from a digital video recording system. This may not follow the methodology of Computer Forensics. The key differences between DCCTV retrieval and a computer forensic investigation are that, with DCCTV retrievals the recording device's operational settings may have to be reconfigured to retrieve the video data, and the entire system's contents may not require a forensic examination. This document is not intended to address Forensic Video Analysis techniques performed after the retrieval of video data.

Recognizing DCCTV Evidence and its Nature

Due to its value in the evidentiary process, as well as its potential value for intelligence and security matters, it is imperative that Law Enforcement recognize, protect and properly collect video from DCCTV systems.

- DCCTV information may exist at a scene or at nearby locations
- Look up, look down, and look around
- DCCTV may be recorded or stored at a remote off-site location

Types of Digital Video Recording Systems (DVRs)

DCCTV systems found in residential, commercial or governmental institutions may include two major types:

- Stand-Alone Embedded Digital Video Recorder
- Personal Computer

Stand-Alone Embedded Digital Video Recorder – replaces the analog VCR and can allow for multiple camera inputs.

Front

Back
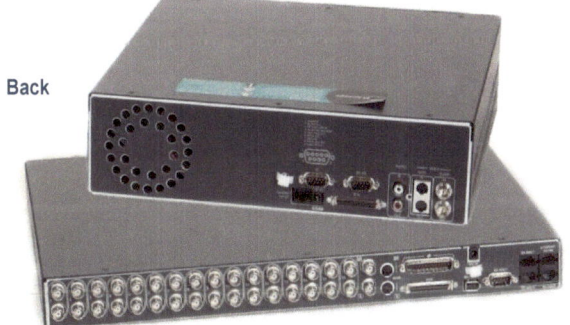

<u>PC-Based Digital Video Recorder</u> – may appear to be a standard computer or may be a proprietary turnkey system with video recording capability.

Front

Back

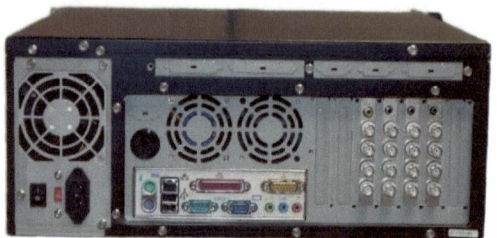

Both systems may have the following:

- Built-in multiplexer
- Transactional data
- Audio recording capabilities
- Other peripheral devices as part of the system
- Network capabilities
- Camera control capabilities
- PC-based systems may also contain business and/or personal data

DVR Recordings

All DVRs utilize compression when recording video data to reduce the amount of storage and transmission requirements. Most digital video recording systems also utilize a native or proprietary file format to record video data. This usually requires a proprietary playback software or special codec from the manufacturer to play back the files, along with any metadata (e.g., time, date, camera number).

In addition to the retrieval of the native/proprietary video files, many systems allow the video data to be downloaded/exported in an "open file format" that will be viewable in a non-proprietary software (e.g., AVI in Windows Media Player or MOV in QuickTime). It should be taken into consideration that these methods often further compress the video data.

Whenever possible, the native/proprietary recorded video file(s) from the DCCTV recording system should be retrieved to maintain the integrity and image quality of the evidence. In addition, consideration should be given to retrieving a non-proprietary video file to facilitate quick viewing.

(This page is intentionally left blank.)

Steps to Take Upon Scene Arrival

- Notes should be kept detailing the methods used and steps taken.

- Determine if a manual is available to assist with system information (e.g., passwords, output options).

- Establish that relevant video has been recorded by reviewing the recording. Preferably, a person with knowledge of the recording device should operate it during playback, if it is appropriate for them to do so.

- Determine the earliest recorded date. This will determine approximately how much time you have to retrieve the data before the system begins to overwrite it.

  ▶ For example, if the earliest recorded date is seven days prior to the incident date, you may have no more than seven days before the relevant data is written over.

- Determine if retrieval can be performed by the venue owner/security system's operator. If yes, will the retrieval be in line with best practices?

- Determine if the DCCTV installer company or a trained operator is available to assist in the retrieval.

- Compare the time displayed by the DCCTV system with the current time. Document the difference, if any. It is suggested that a reference clock be used, such as the Navy Observatory Master Clock at (202) 762-1401 and (202) 762-1069, or NIST Telephone Time of Day Service at (303) 499-7111. These services will provide Universal Time and/or Eastern Time.

- Acquire and document the following information:
  - Digital video recorder make, model and serial number
  - Whether system is PC-based or Stand-Alone Embedded
  - Number of recording units installed
  - Whether system is networked
  - System time and date displayed
  - Actual current date and time (from reference clock)
  - Recording capacity of the system and when it will overwrite
  - Number of camera(s) and the active camera numbers
  - Camera(s) make and model
  - Are any cameras infrared-sensitive and, if so, identify.
  - Multiplexer make and model, if applicable
  - System password
  - System settings
    - Image quality (e.g., high, medium, low)
    - Frames/pictures per second
    - Recorded image/frame size (e.g., 320 x 240)
    - Can it be determined if any cameras are alarm or motion triggered?
    - Number of hard drives; storage capacity of each
    - System firmware version
    - Other available system settings (e.g., event log)
  - Playback software name and version
  - Software password
  - Is audio being recorded? If so, how many channels and are they all downloadable/exportable?

- Acquire and document the following information (*cont.*):
  ▸ Is a copy of the most current maintenance/service log available?
  ▸ Other information of importance
  ▸ Scene contact information
    ◆ Scene address
    ◆ Hours of operation
    ◆ Scene point of contact and telephone number
    ◆ DCCTV system installer point of contact and telephone number
- Photograph system (front and back).
- Sketch DCCTV camera placement and position (See Appendix A-01).
- Remove network cable, if necessary.
- Determine how much data needs to be retrieved.
- Determine the native/proprietary file format the system uses.
- Determine best method for retrieval.

(This page is intentionally left blank.)

Assessing the Recording System for Output

A determination should be made as to how much and what type of data needs to be retrieved from the DCCTV recording device. An evaluation of the system's output options should help determine the best and most practical method of outputting the video. When making this assessment, collection of the native/proprietary video file should remain the highest priority to ensure image quality. Other factors to consider include: the amount of media required, Law Enforcement hours that will be incurred, and the data transfer time.

Examples:

If the incident is a 10-minute robbery, the system has a CD writer and the proprietary file(s) fit on a CD, then collection on CD would be the best method.

If the request is for 24 hours of video and the system has an external USB port, connecting an external USB hard drive may be the best option. This assumes that the system allows for recovery of large amounts of data at one time.

If the request is for 30 days of video, the best, or only, option may be producing a bit-for-bit duplicate of the hard drive(s) and/or removing the recording unit from the scene.

DVR Recording System Outputs (systems may include more than one)

This list is not exhaustive and other methods may exist based on the recording system.

- Compact Disc Rewritable/Digital Versatile Disc Rewritable

- Compact flash
- USB

- IEEE 1394 Firewire/iLink
- Network port

- Analog video
- VGA/DVI output

RCA   S-Video   Composite

- SCSI port (60 pin and 50 pin)

• Removable hard drive

• Magnetic digital data storage
  tape (**DAT**, **DLT**, **DDS**, **AIT**)

• DV cassette drive
  (e.g., Sony HSR-1P)

• Jaz

• Zip

• Magneto Optical

Important:

- Administrative and/or Engineer login access to the DVR usually allows more options for retrieval, including native/proprietary files.

- Time/date stamp with file. You may have to take the downloaded/exported file without the time/date data to ensure the highest quality footage, and take a second retrieval of the footage which includes the time/date data utilizing the output option that may be of lesser quality to ensure you have the information.

- On systems where the time/date stamp can be moved, ensure that this overlay does not obscure critical events.

- Once the appropriate output option is chosen and the video data retrieved, a master should be retained. Depending upon the data retrieval method chosen, additional steps may be needed to create the master.

- The amount of time and storage needed to retrieve the video data may dictate the best method for retrieval.

- Performing a test retrieval will assist in estimating the time and storage requirements for the chosen output option.

14

The intent of "respective order" is to consider the list from beginning to end as being organized from most advisable to least advisable – from a technical and quality of service standpoint.

CD/DVD Writer

Many DCCTV systems have a built-in or external CD/DVD writer to retrieve the recorded video. In some instances, an external CD/DVD writer can also be connected through a USB/Firewire/SCSI port (see USB/Firewire/SCSI Devices).

• Generally, the DCCTV system software will have an archive, backup, copy, or export function in which you can retrieve the data directly to the CD/DVD writer.

• Generally, the system software will allow you to copy the proprietary viewer to the disc while burning, however, you may have to manually select this option.

• Write-once CD-Rs, DVD-Rs, or DVD+Rs should be used.

- Some drives may only write to a specific brand(s) of media. If difficulties are encountered when writing video data, try another brand of media.

- Some DCCTV systems may only take a CD-RW/DVD-RW disc. At the earliest possible time, all data should be transferred from the CD-RW/DVD-RW to a CD-R/DVD-R/DVD+R to create the master evidence.

- The system may require you to format the CD/DVD, either in the DVR itself or in another computer.

- After retrieval, verify that the downloaded/exported file(s) play back correctly on another system, and that the proper dates and times were retrieved.

- If multiple files are retrieved, they should be named to ensure that the proper order of playback is identifiable.

- The resulting produced CD/DVD is the master evidence. If more than one disc is created, each should be identified for proper order of playback.

Compact Flash Drives

Some DCCTV systems have a compact flash card option, which is usually intended for short video sequences and should be used as a temporary storage medium only. Even though many cards now have the ability to hold gigabytes of information, these drives are not as readily available as CD/DVD writers and the cards can be expensive. If video is recovered via these drives, at the earliest possible time, all data should be transferred from the compact flash card to a more permanent media to create the master evidence.

Some systems require an appropriately sized and formatted compact flash card (See the system manual for more information).

Some systems that employ compact flash drives export files in real time (e.g., a 10-minute file will take 10 minutes to download/export). This may not be the most appropriate option for the retrieval of a large amount of data.

USB/Firewire/SCSI Devices

USB/Firewire/SCSI ports can be used to connect external CD/DVD writers, drives, and legacy devices. It should first be established that the port is a working port. Some devices may require activation by installing the necessary drivers on the  recording system. It is recommended that the manufacturer be contacted before attempting to install any drivers.

Example: External USB CD/DVD writers may be used for retrieving smaller amounts of data if no other option exists. External USB/Firewire hard drives are a good resource when large amounts of data need to be collected.

- On some PC based systems that utilize a "standard" Windows operating system, it may be possible to copy the native/proprietary file(s) using Windows Explorer. **NOTE:** This does not work on all systems as the file(s) retrieved in this manner may require the use of the hardware/software during the retrieval process for playback later. It is strongly recommended to know the system before utilizing this method or to consult the manufacturer to ensure the file(s) copied will be capable of playback.

- Most DVR systems have a limitation on the amount of data that can be retrieved (downloaded/exported) at a time, typically 1 GB, sometimes 2GB. This limit may not be specified in the system manual or known to the manufacturer. It is best to keep your file(s) under 1 GB, unless you know for sure it is capable of more.

- Generally, the DCCTV system software will have an archive, backup, copy, or export function in which you can retrieve the data directly to the device you have attached. You may have to chose the device or navigate to it.

- Generally, the system software will allow you to copy the proprietary viewer to the disc while burning, however, you may have to manually select this option.

- After retrieval, verify that the downloaded/exported file(s) play back correctly on another system, and that the proper dates and times were retrieved.

- If multiple files are retrieved, they should be named to ensure that the proper order of playback is identifiable.

- USB/Firewire hard drives are usually considered a temporary storage medium. Therefore, at the earliest possible time, all data should be transferred from the drive to a more permanent media to create the master evidence. The drive should then be wiped before reusing. If the file(s) retrieved are too large, the USB/Firewire drive may be retained as the master evidence.

Network Connection

Many DCCTV recording systems have network ports. Furthermore, many DCCTV systems have their own proprietary "network viewer" software which allows for multi-computer connectivity and recovery of the native/proprietary recorded file(s).

If you do not have any experience with computers or networking, it is highly recommended that you obtain assistance prior to retrieving video data using this method.

By utilizing an ethernet crossover cable, computer, and network viewer, a connection to the DVR can be established and the native/proprietary file(s) downloaded/exported. The remote or network viewer software is installed on a separate computer/laptop, the IP address of the DVR is usually put into the remote viewer software, and a connection is established.

Verify that the network viewer recovers the native/proprietary recorded video file. Example: Some remote viewers only allow for the collection of .JPG or .BMP images and not the entire native/proprietary recorded video file.

- Ensure you have administrator rights on the computer/laptop to which you are downloading/exporting the file(s). Disable any firewalls.

- Screen savers should be disabled as they can interfere and/or disrupt the download/export process (See Appendix A-02).

- **Warning:** Power scheme settings for the computer to which you are downloading/exporting the file(s) should be set to 'always on' with hibernation disabled (See Appendix A-03 and A-04).

- The IP address may be required from the DVR. This usually requires accessing the menu functions of the DVR. Care should be taken not to change other settings on the DVR when doing this.

- If you have to change the IP address on the DVR, make note of the original IP address so you can change it back when you are finished. Changing the IP address may also require rebooting the system.

- Some proprietary remote/network viewers are installed on the DVR system for easy access. Otherwise, searching the vendor's website or contacting the vendor directly may be necessary.

- On some systems, setting up a standard Windows network connection between the computer/laptop and the DVR may be necessary (e.g., computer/laptop 192.168.10.1, and the DVR 192.168.10.2). **NOTE:** It is best practice to try and retain the existing IP settings on the DVR and change those on the computer/laptop to match.

- If a network viewer for the system does not exist, a connection may be possible utilizing Windows Explorer, a web browser, and typing in an appropriate IP address.

- Most DVR systems have a limitation on the amount of data that can be retrieved (downloaded/exported) at a time, typically 1 GB, sometimes 2GB. This limit may not be specified in the system manual or known to the manufacturer. It is best to keep your files under 1 GB, unless you know for sure it is capable of more.

- Some networkable systems may only allow for the video to be "streamed" out and may not provide native/proprietary data transfer. Metadata can be lost through "streaming." Unless this is the only option, it is preferable to output to digital magnetic tape.

- Ensure network speed is sufficient to ensure that no data is lost and to prevent crashes/timeouts during downloading/exporting.

- You may have to disable any firewall installed, ensure you have administrator rights on the DVR. After completing video data retrieval, confirm you have re-enabled the firewall and various settings.

- After retrieval, verify that the downloaded/exported file(s) play back correctly on another system, and that the proper dates and times were retrieved.

- If multiple files are retrieved, they should be named to ensure that the proper order of playback is identifiable.

- Ensure you have also retrieved the proprietary playback software.

- Return all changed system settings to their prior state after data has been retrieved.

- The computer/laptop or USB/Firewire hard drive(s) that you connected to the computer/laptop to retrieve the video file(s), usually are considered a temporary storage medium. Therefore, at the earliest possible time, all data should be transferred from the laptop/USB/Firewire drive to a more permanent media to create the master evidence. If an external hard drive was used, then it should be wiped before reusing. If the file(s) retrieved are too large, the USB/Firewire drive may be retained as the master evidence.

Replacing Hard Drives

In some situations, the quickest solution may appear to be to remove the hard drive(s) from the system and replace them. This option should be considered carefully as there are many factors that come into play. Simply removing a hard drive(s) does not ensure the video files contained on that hard drive(s) will playback. Some DVR systems require the actual DVR hardware to playback the video files on the drive.

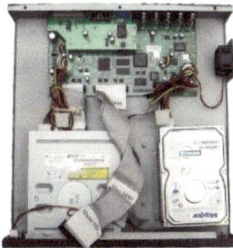
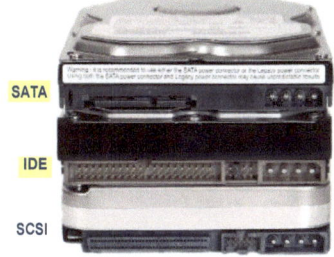

SATA

IDE

SCSI

If you have limited computer hardware experience, consider calling someone for assistance. Care should be taken to follow appropriate health and safety procedures, particularly with regard to potential exposure to electricity.

- The system should be properly shut down prior to removing any hard drive, even if the drive appears to be "hot swappable."
- Ensure that all of the system's hard disc drives are retrieved. The system may have a removable drive in a caddy, but also additional internal drive(s).
- Document the master/slave drive configuration of all retrieved drive(s).
- The DVR may require a specific brand, model and size of hard drive to operate correctly. Consult the manufacturer, manufacturer's web site, or system manual for more information.

- The new drive(s) may need to be formatted by the DVR before it will recognize and record to it.

- Once the new drives are installed, restart the system and confirm that recording and playback are operational, as the system may require that vendor specific software/operating system be installed. Failure to install such software can render a system either partially or completely inoperable.

- If you remove the existing drive(s), be aware that you have removed the archive data stored on the CCTV system.

- The removed hard drive(s) is the master evidence. If more than one hard drive is removed, each should be properly identified.

Drive Duplication

In some situations, drive duplication may be necessary. This option should be considered carefully as there are many factors that come into play. Drive duplication does not ensure playback. Some DVR systems require the original hard drive(s) for playback.

It is recommended that a bit for bit duplicate of the original hard drive(s) be produced, not an image set.

- The system should be properly shut down prior to removing any hard drive, even if the drive appears to be "hot swappable."

- Some systems require the original hard drive(s) for proper operation. Therefore, if the drive(s) is duplicated, place the duplicated drive back in the system, make sure the system is operational, and retrieve the original drive(s) from the scene. If the system is not operational, the recording device may have to be retrieved, along with the original hard drive(s).

- Ensure you duplicate all the drives in the system as the DVR may have internal drives.

- Document the master/slave drive configuration of all duplicated drives.

- External playback software may exist to access the video data on the duplicate hard drive.

- Upon initial inspection, a hard drive duplicated from a system may not appear to contain data when viewed using a standard PC. Many systems utilize proprietary formats that prevent data from being recognized. If you don't see files upon inspection of the duplicate drive, don't assume that nothing has been recorded.

- The duplicate drive(s) and/or original drive(s) should be inspected using a write blocker and a separate computer/laptop.

- The duplicated drive(s) and/or original drive(s) retrieved from the scene are considered the evidentiary master from which working copies may be produced.

Legacy Output

The following output methods usually enable retrieval of the native/proprietary video data and can be located inside the digital recording unit or as an attached external device. In some circumstances, this may be the only method available on the DVR system for retrieval of the video data. Retrieval and playback may require additional steps. These can typically be connected through the SCSI port. Do not discount this as a retrieval method if you do not have these devices.

- DDS TAPE (Digital Data Storage)
- Iomega Jaz
- Iomega Zip
- Floppy
- Magneto Optical

Except for DDS Tape, the above media should be considered a temporary medium. At the earliest possible time, all data should be transferred to a more permanent media to create the master evidence.

NOTE: It may not be possible to duplicate DDS cassettes; where possible consider uploading to the DVR and downloading/exporting the relevant portion to a more readily accessible medium and one capable of duplication.

Removal of DVR Unit

In circumstances where the above listed options have been determined to be either impractical or impossible, the decision may be made to remove the recording unit itself.

This assumes that it is physically possible to do so, and that the removal is justified. For example, where the volume of data required is very large, it may be time efficient to temporarily remove the recorder and perform the retrieval in the lab, rather than on site. Alternatively, there may be no method for extracting the video data (e.g., CD writer or USB ports) and it may be necessary to remove the recorder and retain the unit as the evidentiary master.

- The recording device should be stopped and the system properly shut down prior to removal.
- Ensure all relevant components of the system are collected (e.g., power supply, remote control, dongle, manual, cables).
- Ensure all cables are uniquely identified (e.g., camera inputs) to facilitate reinstallation of the system.
- If no other method exists for extracting the video data from the DVR recording device retrieved from the scene, the DVR is considered the evidentiary master.

Non Native/Proprietary Data Retrieval

Although they record digitally, some DCCTV systems only have an analog output. For these systems, consideration should be given to collection of the DVR system as the master evidence. If this is not practical, then the following should be considered:

S-Video/Composite Output

- Video can only be retrieved in "real time" and the process should be repeated for each required camera view.

- When a system has both an s-video and composite output, it is recommended that the s-video be used.

S-Video   Composite

- It is recommended that a digital video tape recorder (VTR) be utilized. Some examples of digital VTRs are Digital Betacam, DVC Pro, DVCam, Mini DV, and Digital 8.

- The video recording should be collected to digital magnetic tape.

- Ensure the "time/date stamp" is displayed on output; this may require checking several signals (e.g., composite and s-video).

- It is recommended that the DVR output be directly connected to the VTR and a separate output from the VTR be made to a monitor to ensure that the signal is being received and recorded.

- Prior to recording the video data, check playback speed on the DVR.

- The collection of video data to VHS tape or Video DVD should be considered a last resort and conducted if it is the only possible option.

- Taking the analog output from a DVR may produce a different frame size from the original native/proprietary file recorded frame size.

- The produced magnetic tape is considered the evidentiary master.

NOTE: Video capture cards can be utilized for digitizing a video signal from the DVR into a computer. Most capture cards can take an s-video and composite input, while higher quality cards can input a component, SDI, and/or HD video input. It is recommended that the highest quality input be utilized. Care should be taken to ensure that the recorded frame size is maintained when utilizing this method. The digitized data should be captured as uncompressed (1:1) and retained as the master evidence.

VGA/DVI Output

Some DCCTV systems have a VGA or DVI output that allows the video data to be displayed on a computer monitor. These outputs can be converted to a video signal, usually analog, through the use of a scan converter. This video signal could then be recorded to video format and retained as the evidentiary master. This method typically reduces the image quality below that of an s-video/composite output and should be considered a last resort.

- Do not change the time and date on the DVR system.

- It is not recommended that any additional software be installed on the DVR system (e.g., CD writing software, if it is not present). If it is absolutely necessary to install additional software, it is highly recommended that the manufacturer be contacted prior to installation.

- If it is determined that the video data of interest has been overwritten, check to see if the venue retains back up files.

- Administrative/Engineer access to the DVR usually allows more options for retrieval, including native/proprietary files.

- Time/date stamp with file. You may have to take the downloaded/exported file without the time/date data to ensure the highest quality footage, and take a second retrieval of the footage which includes the time/date data utilizing the output option that may be of lesser quality to ensure you have the information.

- On systems where the time/date stamp can be moved, ensure that this overlay does not obscure critical events.

- A review of the live monitor is not sufficient and may appear to be of better quality than the actual recorded video.

- Whenever possible, the system should remain recording during the retrieval of the video data.

- Many digital video recording systems allow you to auto copy the proprietary playback viewer while retrieving the video data. This should always be done when available. If the system does not allow this, steps should be taken to retrieve the correct version, with full functionality, required for playback/viewing.

- The native/proprietary video data should be retrieved. If time permits, and if the system downloads/exports a file that is in a non proprietary format (e.g., AVI) for quick viewing, consider collecting that as well as the native/proprietary.

- If the DVR has multi camera capabilities, all the video data for the required area of interest should be taken as it was recorded. These cameras should be recorded in isolation, showing one camera full screen and not multi cameras on a single screen (e.g., not 4, 8, and 16 on a single screen).

- Ensure that the frame rate upon retrieval is as near to recorded frame rate as possible.

- Ensure that the aspect ratio of the video data upon retrieval is as near to the recorded aspect ratio as possible.

- Working copies may be produced from the master evidence.

Evidence Handling Procedures

- To provide an audit trail, contemporaneous notes should be recorded detailing the course of actions taken.
- Initiate a chain of custody for the retrieved evidence, per agency policies.
- If transport of evidence is required, ensure the evidence is packaged and sealed appropriately based on the media (e.g., jewel cases for compact discs, anti static bags and individual foam insert boxes for hard drives).
- Keep evidence away from magnets, excessive temperatures, and otherwise hostile environments.

(This page is intentionally left blank.)

Prior to Leaving Scene, Ensure That

- You have completed all the necessary documentation.
- You have collected all required video data.
- The retrieved video data plays back correctly, preferably on another system, and that the proper dates and times were retrieved.
- The proprietary playback software, network viewer, backup player, and/or archive software have been retrieved.
- The recording system has been returned to its original state (e.g., any changes to the system settings have been reset).
- The recording system has been verified as operational.
- If removing the recording system, ensure that all necessary peripherals have been retrieved.
- If you have retrieved the recording system, have legal implications been considered?

(This page is intentionally left blank.)

Legal Issues

- Some DCCTV systems are used as both a DCCTV recording system as well as a business computer. This should be considered when it is necessary to remove the digital video recording system from the scene.

- Consideration should be given as to whether owner consent is necessary and applicable for removing the recording system.

- Ensure the scope of the search warrant encompasses the video data and necessary system components.

- Is it necessary or feasible to provide the business with a replacement recording device if their system has been removed?

- If you need to retrieve or replace the recording device's hard drive(s), will you be voiding an existing warranty on the system? If yes, have you received the proper level of authorization?

- If the DCCTV system is an instrumentality or fruit of the offense, seize it.

(This page is intentionally left blank.)

Recommended Equipment Needed

To enable retrieval from a variety of systems that will be encountered, a range of equipment is recommended. The following is a suggested list of equipment that should permit video data retrieval from the most commonly encountered systems:

- Laptop with:
  - CD/DVD writable drives
  - USB ports
  - Network port
  - Firewire ports
  - Wireless access
  - Capability for installing proprietary viewers – ensure you are Administrator on this computer and there are no restrictions that would impede the download (e.g., firewalls, agency software)
- Media card reader (multi-format)
- USB floppy drive
- Four port network switch/hub
- External CD/DVD writeable drive – USB/SCSI/Firewire
- USB and Firewire storage devices in multiple sizes
- IDE, SCSI and SATA hard drives in multiple sizes (80, 160, 300 GB)
- Cables to include:
  - Network cables (crossover cable and straight patch cable)
  - Composite and s-video cables, as well as RCA to BNC adapters
  - Audio cables (RCA, stereo, and mono mini)

- Cables to include (*cont.*):
  - ‣ USB cables
  - ‣ Firewire cables (iLink, 400, 800)
  - ‣ Power cables
  - ‣ Extension cords
- Write blockers (IDE, Firewire)
- Blank Media (CD-R, DVD-R, DVD+R, DVD-Ram, CD-RW, DVD-RW, DVD+RW)
- Blank compact flash cards in varying sizes
- Video monitor (NTSC/PAL)
- Computer monitor
- Still camera with extra film or media
- Too kit containing :
  - ‣ Flashlight
  - ‣ Anti-static strap
  - ‣ Mirror
  - ‣ Assorted screwdrivers
  - ‣ Pens
  - ‣ Permanent marker (appropriate for marking media)
- Digital Video Tape Recorder
- Analog Video Tape Recorder
- Magnetic tapes (analog/digital)
- Appropriate forms (chain of custody, notes, consent)
- Appropriate evidence packaging (anti static bags, jewel cases)

Example of Site Plan for Convenience Store

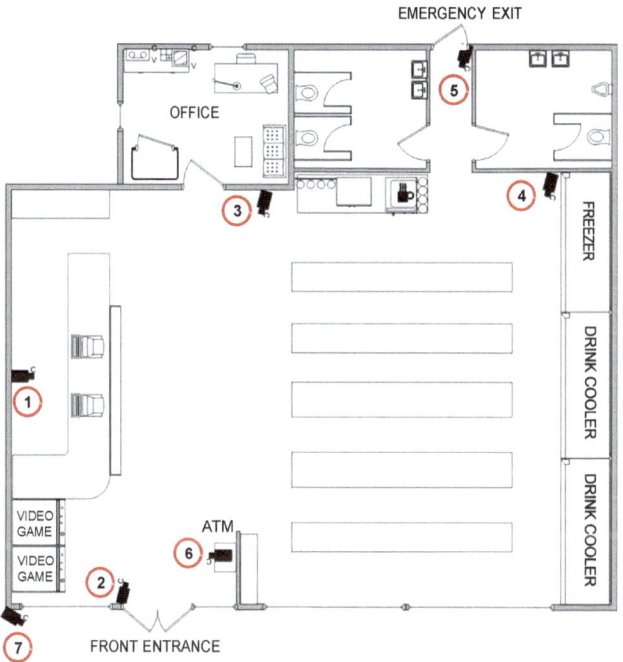

Camera 1: Clerk and check-out area, facing east
Camera 2: Front door entrance, facing north
Camera 3: Outside of office, facing south
Camera 4: Freezer area, facing south
Camera 5: Emergency exit, facing south
Camera 6: Automated teller machine, facing west
Camera 7: Parking lot, facing south-east

Taken from the Scientific Working Group on Imaging Technology (SWGIT) document, Section 4 *"Recommendations and Guidelines for Using Closed-Circuit Television Security Systems in Commercial Institutions."*

Display Properties

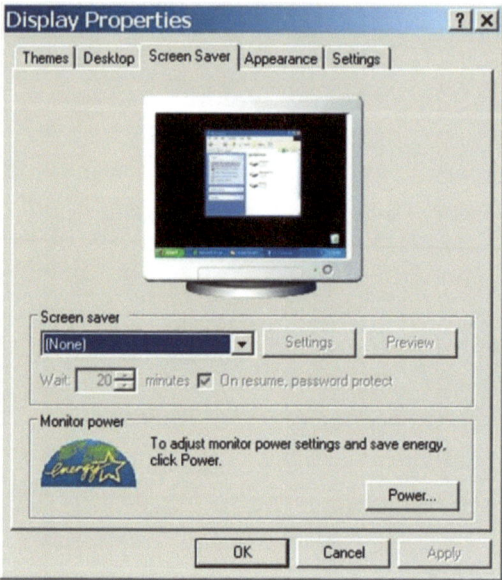

- To access these options, refer to the system manual.
- The setting should be set as above.

Power Options Properties

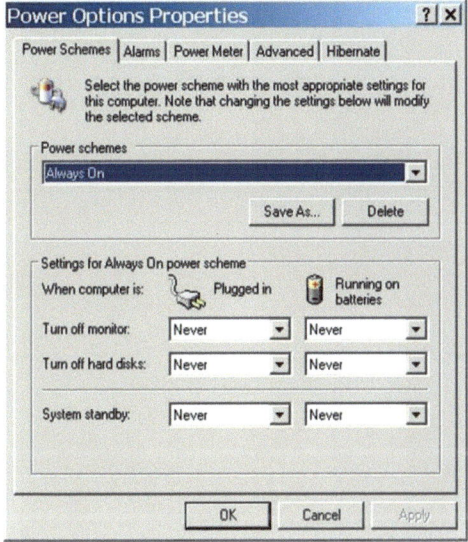

• To access these options, refer to the system manual.

• The settings should be set as above.

Power Options Properties

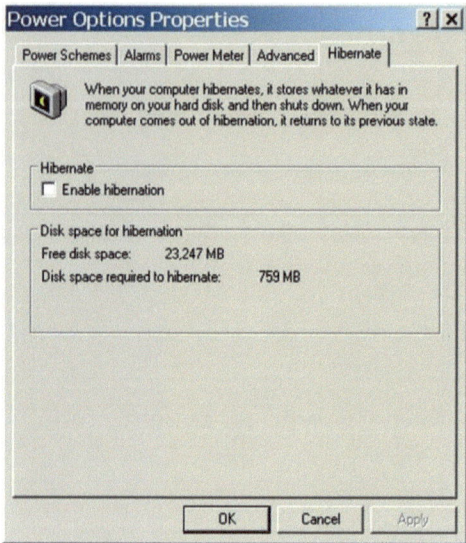

•To access these options, refer to the system manual.

•Enable Hibernation should NOT be checked.

Glossary

Analog Output	A mechanism to output a video signal to a television monitor or recording device.
AIT	Advanced Intelligent Tape. A format for storing and backing up data on magnetic tape.
.AVI	Audio Video Interleaved. A sound and motion picture file format that was developed by Microsoft. For the purpose of DCCTV, AVI files can require a proprietary software or codec for playback of the retrieved video data.
Bit	Binary Digit. The smallest unit of information on a machine.
Bit for Bit Duplicate	An accurate and complete reproduction of all data objects independent of the physical media.
.BMP	Short for BitMap; a 24 bit Windows graphic file format. A standard for bit-mapped graphics format and is Microsoft's preferred format for graphics. For the purpose of DCCTV, some DCCTV systems allow you to save still images to a .BMP file format.
Caddy	A device for moving, carrying or holding an item.
CCTV	Closed Circuit Television. Used in surveillance and security applications.

CD/DVD	Compact Disc/Digital Versatile Disc. Optical disc storage media used to store digital data. Both CD's and DVD's come in write once and rewritable form (e.g. CD-R and CD-RW).
CD/DVD Writer	An internal or external drive that allows for playback of stored data and writing of data on a CD or DVD.
Chain of Custody	The chronological documentation of the movement, location and possession of evidence.
Codec	Refers to a device or program capable of encoding and decoding digital data. Codecs encode a stream or signal for transmission, storage or encryption and decode it for viewing. For the purpose of DCCTV, codecs are usually proprietary and may be required for playback of the retrieved video data.
Compact Flash	Removable media data storage device that typically uses flash memory.
Component Video Signal	An analog signal that represents a part of the composite signal. In a component signal these elements include Y (luminance), R-Y, and B-Y (the color difference signals), or the red, green and blue signals separately. The R, G, B, color signals are sent through three separate coaxial cables.
Composite Video Signal	An analog signal which contains chroma, video, blanking and sync information and has been combined using one of the coding standards NTSC, PAL, SECAM, etc. Signal sent through one coaxial cable.

Computer Forensics	The scientific examination, analysis, and/or evaluation of digital evidence in legal matters.
DAT	Digital Audio Tape. Magnetic tape recording and playback medium developed initially for audio signals. Can also be used for the recording and playback of video.
Data	Information in analog or digital form that can be transmitted or processed.
DCCTV	Digital Closed Circuit Television. Used in surveillance and security applications.
DCCTV Retrieval	The process of retrieving data from digital CCTV systems.
DDS	Digital Data Storage. A format for storing and backing up data on magnetic tape.
DLT	Digital Linear Tape. A format for storing and backing up data on magnetic tape.
Dongle	Electronic key or license to control a specific software application or piece of hardware.
Downloading /Exporting	(V) The process of retrieving audio, video, still images and transactional data from a DVR system. Can be either in the native/proprietary format or an open format.

DVI	Digital Video Interface. A digital interface standard created to convert analog signals into digital signals to accommodate both analog and digital monitors.
DVR	Digital Video Recorder. A stand alone embedded system or a PC based system.
File Format	The structure by which data is organized in a file.
Firewire	An interface port between a computer and a device, that allows for fast data transfer, also known as IEEE 1394. Some Firewire devices include: an external hard drive and cd/dvd writers.
Floppy Disk	A removable data storage device that is made of a disk of thin, flexible magnetic medium. Requires a floppy drive to retrieve the data.
Format	(V) To prepare a storage media, usually a disk, for reading and writing. (N) One or several combined elements that may be used to describe the video recording method. These include tape width (e.g. 8 mm, 1/2 inch, 3/4 inch, 1 inch), signal form (e.g. composite, Y/C, component), media (e.g. VHS tape, DVD, CD), data storage type (e.g. analog/digital, AVI/MOV/MPEG), and signal standard (e.g. NTSC, PAL, SECAM).
HD	High Definition. A high resolution television video signal.

Hot Swappable	A drive that has the ability to be removed or replaced in a machine while the machine remains operating and without rebooting.
IDE	Integrated Drive Electronics. An interface used as a data path or bus for a disk storage device.
iLink	A serial bus interface standard between a personal computer and digital video and audio devices, offering high speed communication between the devices. ilink is Sony's implementation of the standard. ilink uses only four pins rather than six, discarding the two pins that provide power to the device.
Image Set	An accurate and complete reproduction of all data objects, independent of the physical media, that are saved as files.
IP Address	Internet Protocol Address. An IP address is a 32 bit number that identifies either the sender or the receiver of information. This information is sent in packets across the network and each machine on the network has a unique IP address to identify it.
Jaz	A removable disk storage media introduced by Iomega. Requires a Jaz drive to read the data.
.JPG	A file format that stores a photographic image in a compressed form. For the purpose of DCCTV, some DCCTV systems allow you to save still images to a .jpg file format.

Legacy	Refers to systems that are no longer produced or rarely used.
Magneto Optical	An optical disc capable of having data written and rewritten to it. They can come in the 5.25" or 3.5" format. Requires a magneto optical drive to read the disc.
Master Evidence	The original retrieved data irrespective of media. (e.g. if the recorded video from the DVR hard drive was downloaded to CD/DVD, that CD/DVD is defined as the master).
Master/Slave	A communication protocol where one device has unidirectional control over another. Once a master/slave relationship between devices is established, the direction of control is always from the master to the slave(s). Commonly referred to for hard drive configuration.
Media	Material on which data can be stored.
Metadata	Data, frequently embedded within a file, that describes a file or directory. Can include the location where the content is stored, dates and times, application specific information, and permissions.
.MOV	Video file extension for QuickTime which is a multimedia development, storage, and playback technology from Apple. QuickTime files combine sound, text, animation and video in a single file.

Multiplexer/ Demultiplexer	A device used to combine multiple video signals into a single signal or separate a combined signal. These devices are frequently used in security and law enforcement applications for recording and/or displaying multiple camera images simultaneously or in succession.
Native File Format	The original form of a file. A file created with one application can often be read by others, but a file's native format remains the format it was given by the application that created it. In most DCCTV systems the specific attributes of the video file(s) are proprietary to the program that created it.
Network Port	An interface that provides the capability to link devices for the exchange of information.
Proprietary File Format	See Native File Format.
Proprietary Software	Manufacturer specific computer software necessary to playback the retrieved native/proprietary video data.
Removable Hard Drive	A hard drive that usually is in an enclosure, often with a lock.
SATA	Serial Advanced Technology Attachment. An interface used as a data path or bus for a disk storage device.
Scan converter	An electronic device which converts a computer's video signal to the requirements for NTSC or PAL video so that it can be viewed on a video monitor or recorded to a VCR.

SCSI	Small Computer System Interface. An interface used as a data path or bus for a disk storage device.
SDI	Serial Digital Interface. A standard for digital video transmission over coaxial cable.
Streaming	(V) For the purpose of DCCTV, the process of retrieving the video/audio data while it is being played back.
S-Video Signal	A signal in which the luminance and chrominance information are recorded separately.
Temporary Medium	Any media or device on which data is temporarily stored until transferred to permanent or archival storage.
USB	Universal Serial Bus. An interface used as a data path or bus for connecting to an external device.
VGA	Video Graphic Array. Developed by IBM for displaying video at 640 x 480 by connecting a computer's output to a monitor.
Video	The electronic representation of a sequence of images, depicting either stationary or moving scenes. May contain audio.
VTR	Video Tape Recorder. A device that records a video/audio signal to magnetic tape.

Wiped   To erase all data on digital media by
                        overwriting. This will overwrite all
                        formatting structures and data.

Working copy   A copy or duplicate of a recording or data
                        made from the master evidence or at the
                        same time as the master, that can be used
                        for subsequent viewing, analysis or
                        processing.

Write Blocker   Hardware and/or software methods of
                        preventing modification of media content.

Zip   A removable disk storage media introduced
                        by Iomega. Requires a ZIP drive to read the
                        data.

www.ingramcontent.com/pod-product-compliance
Lightning Source LLC
Chambersburg PA
CBHW040920180526
45159CB00002BA/543